Silver Burdett
SCIENCE

GEORGE G. MALLINSON
Distinguished Professor
of Science Education
Western Michigan University

JACQUELINE B. MALLINSON
Associate Professor of Science
Western Michigan University

WILLIAM L. SMALLWOOD
Head, Science Department
The Community School
Sun Valley, Idaho

CATHERINE VALENTINO
Former Director of Instruction
North Kingstown School Department
North Kingstown, Rhode Island

SILVER BURDETT COMPANY
MORRISTOWN, NEW JERSEY
Atlanta, GA • Cincinnati, OH • Dallas, TX • Northfield, IL • San Carlos, CA • Agincourt, Ontario

THE SILVER BURDETT ELEMENTARY SCIENCE PROGRAM

1–6 Pupils Books
Teachers Editions Levels K–6

Silver Burdett
SCIENCE

Contents

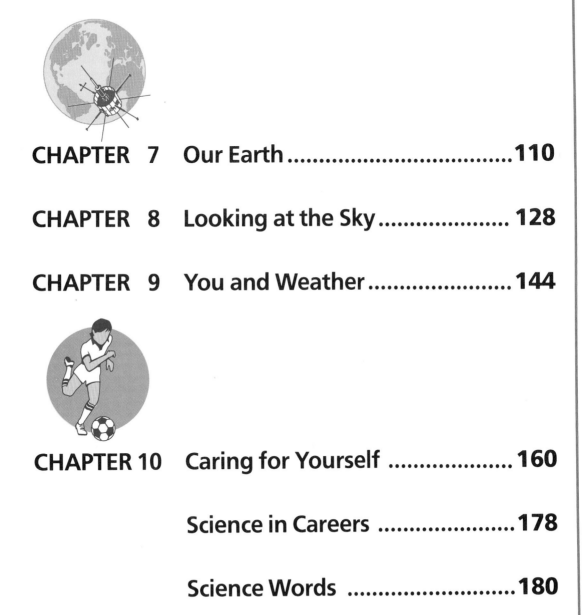

The Adventure of Science

What is Science?

B

What Will I Learn in Science?

How Does Science Help Me?

I use science every day.

Don't Cry Over Spilled Milk

How can I think like a scientist?

I can clean up a spill.

Hide and Go Seek

What is happening?

F

What is the squirrel doing?

Why?

What will the squirrel do next?

G

H

What is happening here?

What will happen next?

1

J

1

Learning About Our World

You have five senses.

1

You use your senses
    to see
    to hear
    to smell
    to taste
    to feel.

You use your eyes to see.
You can see near and far.

How do things look close and far away?

Look at a rock.

Place the rock far away.

Look at the rock again.

How does seeing close and far help you?

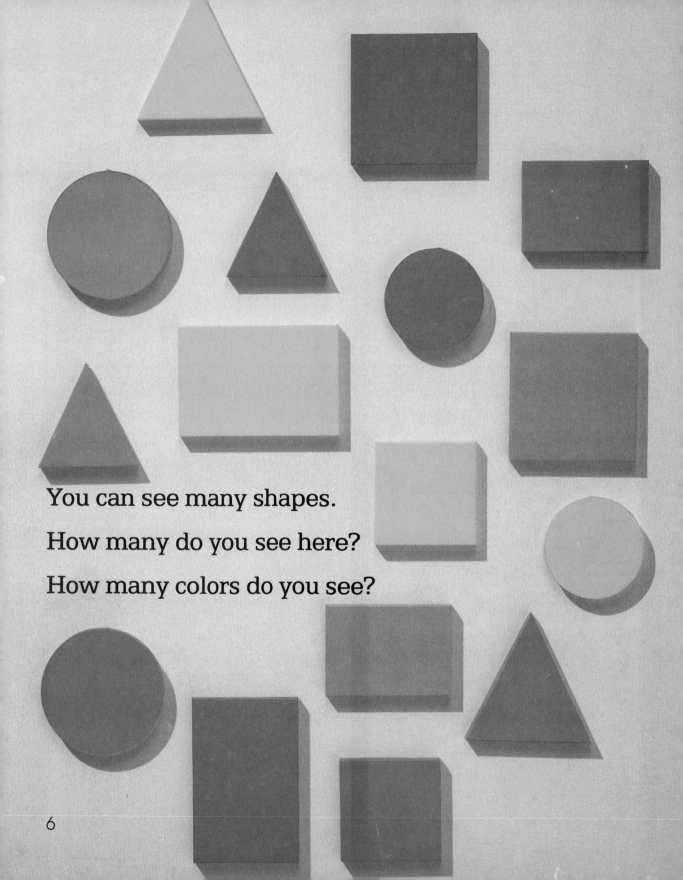

You can see many shapes.

How many do you see here?

How many colors do you see?

Animals also use eyes to see.

Find the eyes on each animal.

You use your ears to hear.

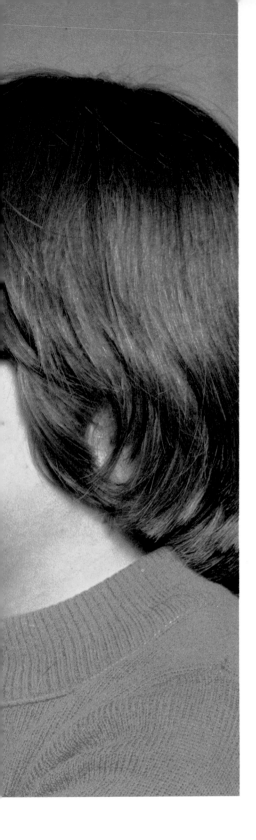

There are many different sounds.
Some sounds are loud.

Some sounds are soft.

What can sounds tell you?

What sounds do you hear?

Where is the sound coming from?

Point to the sound.

How do sounds help us learn?

Animals also use ears to hear.

Find the ears on each animal.

You use your nose to smell.

Some things smell good.
Some things smell bad.
How do these things smell?

What can smelling tell you?

Name the foods you smell.

How many do you know?

How can your nose help you learn?

14

Animals also use a nose to smell.

Find the nose on each animal.

You use your tongue to taste.

Foods have different tastes.

How do these foods taste?

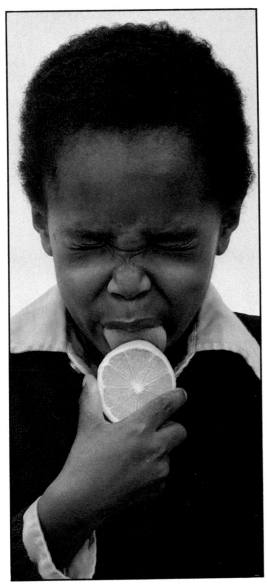

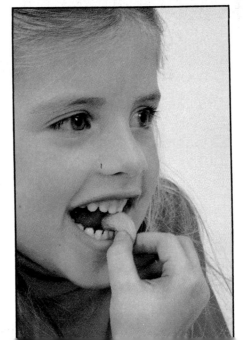

You use your skin to feel.
Some things feel cold.
Some things feel warm.

Find the things that feel hard.
Find the things that feel soft.

Some things feel hard.
Some things feel soft.

19

Some things feel rough.
Some things feel smooth.
Find the things that feel rough.
Find the things that feel smooth.

What can touching tell you?

Feel different things.

How many did you know?

How does touching help you learn?

WORDS TO KNOW

Tell about these things.
Use these words.

shape   color   smooth   rough

   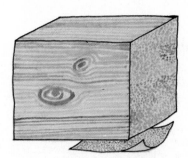

Read each sentence.
Say the missing word.

I see with my ____.

I hear with my ____.

I feel with my ____.

I smell with my ____.

I taste with my ____.

IDEAS TO KNOW

What do your senses tell you?

USING IDEAS

Your senses keep you safe.

How are senses helping here?

2

Many Kinds of Plants

There are many kinds of plants.
How are these plants the same?
How are they different?

Some plants are big.
Some plants are small.

Plants have many shapes.

Plants also have many colors.

What colors do you see here?

Many plants have three main parts.

They have roots.

They have stems.

They have leaves.

The boy is holding a plant.

Find the three main parts.

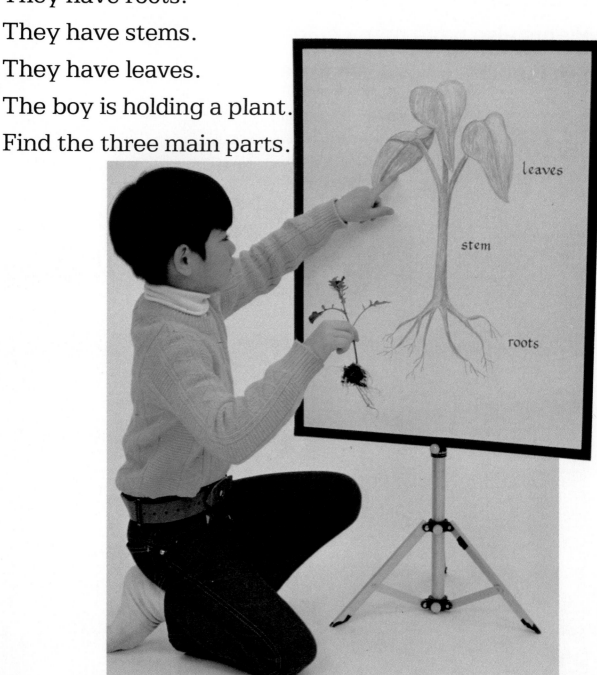

The roots of these plants are different.

How are they different?

Leaves are different shapes.
Leaves are different sizes.
How are these leaves different?

Stems can be long or short.
Stems can be soft or hard.
How are these stems different?

How are leaves alike?

Look at some leaves.

Find leaves that look the same.

Put them in groups.

How is each group different?

How is each group alike?

What other groups can you make?

Plants need some things to live.
Most plants need soil to grow.
They need air and water.
Most plants need light.

Some plants grow indoors.

They need special care.

How is this child taking care of the plant?

33

Many plants grow from seeds.

Each kind of plant has its own kind of seed.

Different plants grow from different seeds.

What will happen to different seeds?

Plant two kinds of seeds.

Give them water.

Check them.

What happened?

Why did some seeds grow faster?

Plants grow in many places.

Some plants grow in soil.

Other plants grow in water.

Look at the pictures.

How are these places different?

Some plants grow in strange places.
Where are these plants growing?

People use plants for food.

Can you name these foods?

People use plants to make things.

What plants do you see here?

How do people use these plants?

Check It Now

WORDS TO KNOW

What are these things?

Match the pictures with the words.

stem   roots   leaves

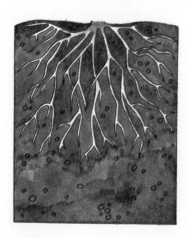

Read each sentence.

Say the missing word.

air   seeds   soil   water   light

Many plants grow from ____.

Most seeds grow in ____.

Most plants need ____ and ____.

The sun gives plants ____.

40

IDEAS TO KNOW

How does a seed grow?

What picture is missing?

Which things come from plants?

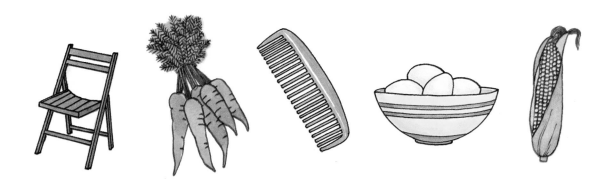

THINKING LIKE A SCIENTIST

Plants we do not want are weeds.

How can we keep weeds from growing?

3

Many Kinds of Animals

There are many kinds of animals.
How are these animals different?

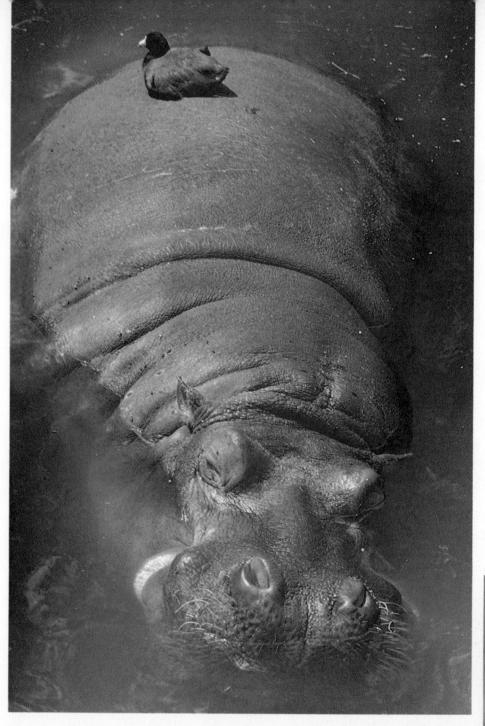

Some animals are big.

Some animals are small.

Which animals are big?

Which animals are small?

Some animals have fur.
Some animals have feathers.

Some animals have a hard shell.

Which animals here have a hard shell?

What do the other animals have?

Animals can move.

They move in many ways.

Some animals run.

Some animals hop.

Some animals swim.

Other animals fly.

Some animals move in other ways.

How do these animals move?

Many baby animals look like their parents.

Do these babies look like their parents?

How are they the same?

How are they different?

These baby animals do not look like their parents.

How are they different?

Animals eat many things.

Some animals eat plants.

Some animals eat other animals.

What are these animals eating?

Animals catch food in many ways.

How are these animals catching their food?

Animals need more than food.
They need water to drink.
Some animals live in the water.

Animals need air.

Most animals need air to breathe.

Some animals move in the air.

Animals need a place to live.

They live in many kinds of places.

Where do these animals live?

What do pet fish need to live?

Make a home for a fish.

How will you care for the fish?

Some animals make good pets.

People must take care of pets.

How are people taking care of these pets?

People use animals in different ways.

We get food from animals.

We also get clothing from animals.

Some animals do work.

How are these animals helping?

What are some ways to group animals?

Cut out pictures of animals.

Put the pictures into groups.

Check It Now

WORDS TO KNOW

How do these animals move?

      hop   walk   fly   run   swim

What body covering does each have?

      fur   skin   shell   feathers

IDEAS TO KNOW

Look at the animals in each group.

Tell how they are alike.

Tell how they are different.

THINKING LIKE A SCIENTIST

How can we tell where an animal lives?

We can look for clues.

There are clues in this picture.

What animals might live near here?

4

Using Colors, Shapes, and Sizes

You use colors.

You use shapes.

You use sizes.

You use them to tell about things.

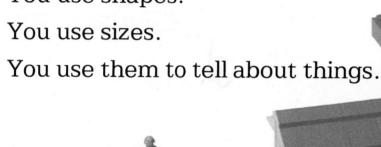

You can see many colors.

Colors help you learn.

They help you tell about things.

The hats in the picture are different.

How are they different?

Look at the picture.

What things are the same color?

Name things that are different colors.

What happens when you mix colors?

Mix some colors.

Try different colors.

What new colors can you make?

What will the blue color do?

Which one will be a darker color?

You can see shapes.

You can feel shapes.

You can use shapes.

Shapes help you learn.

What shapes do you see in the picture?

Look at the picture.

Name things that have the same shape.

Name things that have different shapes.

What shapes make this rocket?

What can you make with shapes?

Put some shapes together.

What did you make?

71

Some things are big.

Some things are small.

Sizes help you learn about things.

They help you tell about things.

Tell about the shoes.

How are they different?

Clothes come in different sizes.

People are different sizes.

Look at the pictures.

How does the hat fit?

How does the dress fit?

Some things are tall.

Some things are short.

Look at the pictures.

Which animal is taller?

BE CAREFUL.
SOME SNAKES
ARE HARMFUL.

Some snakes are long.

Some snakes are longer.

How tall are you?

How can you use straws to find out?

Guess how many straws you will need.

How can straws tell how tall things are?

Get some straws.

Show how tall things are.

Tape your straws on a chart.

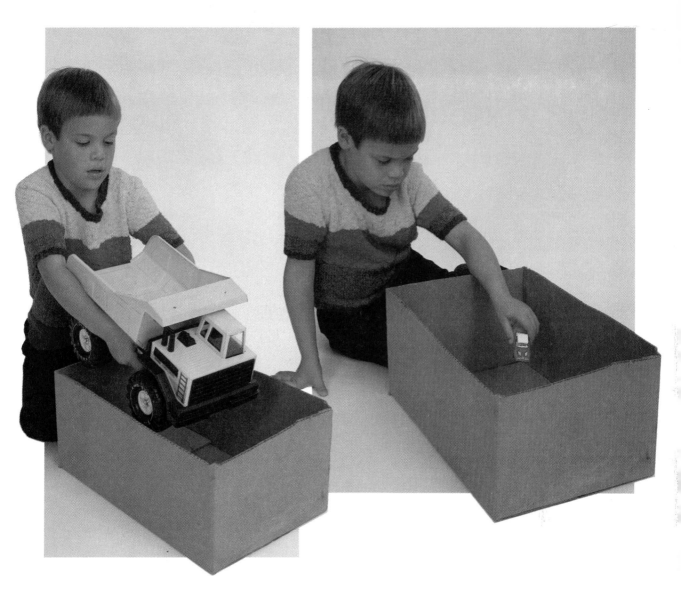

Things take up space.

Some things take up a lot of space.

Some things take up less space.

What is in the boxes?

Which one takes up the most space?

Check It Now

WORDS TO KNOW

How are the trucks alike?

How are the trucks different?

Read each sentence.

Say the missing word.

The is ____.

The  is ____.

The  is ____.

The is ____.

IDEAS TO KNOW

Mix the colors.

⬤ + ⬤ =

⬜ + ⬛ =

▲ + △ =

What shapes do you see?

USING IDEAS

Make a ruler.

Mark 10 centimeters.

What can you measure?

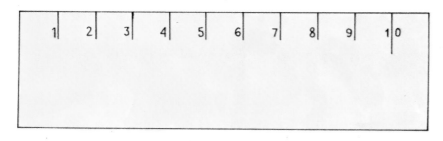

| 1 | 2 | 3 | 4 | 5 | 6 | 7 | 8 | 9 | 10 |

5

Living and Not Living

Look at the pictures.
Which things are living?
Which things are not living?

Animals are living things.
Plants are living things.
People are living things.
Living things grow.

Trees are living things that grow.

These pictures show the same tree.

How do you know this tree grew?

Are these things living?

Will they grow?

Things that are not living do not grow.

Many living things can move on their own.

Animals are living things that move.

Most birds can fly.

Dogs can run.

Some insects can hop.

Many things cannot move on their own.

They need help to move from place to place.

These things are not living.

What helps these things move?

Is a cup a living thing?

Can a cup move by itself?

Tape a penny inside a cup.

Hold the cup on its side on a table.

Keep the penny-side up.

Let go of the cup.

What happens?

How can nonliving things move?

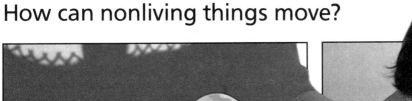

Plants and animals need many things to live.

They need food to help them grow.

They also need air and water.

Look at the picture.

What living things do you see?

What do they need to live?

Do plants need water to grow?

Get two plants that are alike.

Put both plants in sunlight.

Water one plant.

Do not water the other.

What happens if a plant is not watered?

Things that are not living can be anywhere.

A rock is not living.

These are moon rocks.

They do not need food, air, or water.

Living things make new living things.

Plants make seeds.

Seeds grow into new plants.

Dogs have puppies.

Birds lay eggs.

Baby birds hatch from eggs.

What living things are near your school?

How many can you find?

Make a chart to show them.

Which is largest?

Which is smallest?

Where can living things be found?

Check It Now

WORDS TO KNOW

Read each sentence.

Say the missing word.

grow   rock   eggs

Baby birds hatch from ____.

Food, air, and water are not needed by a ____.

Living things ____.

Look at each row.

Which picture does not belong?

IDEAS TO KNOW

Look at the picture.

How many living things can you find?

How many things are not living?

Which number is greater?

THINKING LIKE A SCIENTIST

This plant is a living thing.   This plastic plant is not.

How can you tell the difference?

6

Moving Things

Many things move.

They move in different ways.

How can you move?

How do these things move?

We can see when things are moved.

They are in different places.

Look at the two pictures.

What things are in different places?

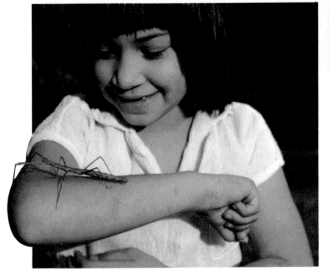

We can feel things move.

Which child can feel things move?

We can hear things move.

Can this boy tell the chair is moving?

Things move in many ways.

Some things move up and down.

Some things roll and spin.

Some things float.

How do these things move?

What makes a pinwheel move?

Look at the pictures.

Make a pinwheel.

Blow on it.

How does it move?

How can you make it move faster?

Things move at different speeds.
Some things move fast.
Some things move slowly.
How do these things move?

People move things in different ways.

They can push or pull things.

Sometimes they lift things.

How is the girl moving the dog?

Machines help us move things.
These are simple machines.

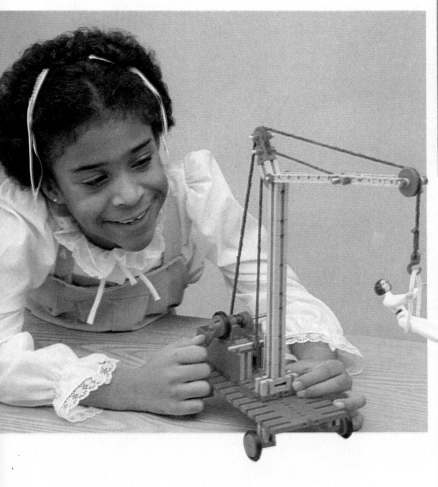

How do these machines help to move things?

Machines help us do work.

They make work easier.

How are these machines helping?

How can you move things?

Make a machine with wheels.

What work does it do?

What things can it move?

How can you make it better?

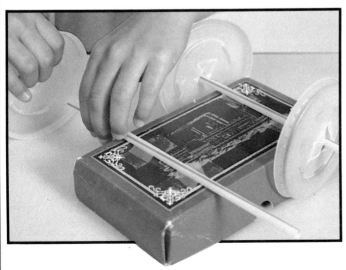

107

Check It Now

WORDS TO KNOW

How do they move things?

Match the pictures with the words.

lift   push   pull   machine

Read each sentence.

Say the missing word.

rolls   spins   floats   flies   crawls

The 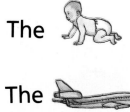 ____.   The ____.

The ____.   The ____.

The ____.

IDEAS TO KNOW

What makes these things move?

Look at the pictures.

Tell how you use each machine.

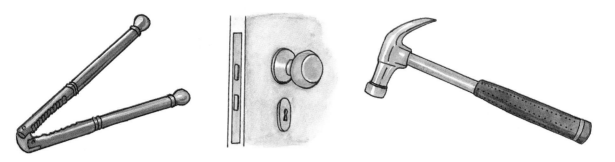

THINKING LIKE A SCIENTIST

What work is being done here?

7

Our Earth

The earth has land.

The earth has water.

The earth has air.

What things do you see in the pictures?

The earth is round.

It is shaped like a ball.

A globe looks like the earth.

How are these other things like the earth?

The earth looks like this from space.

Can you see the water?

Can you see the land?

What else do you see?

The land is made of rocks and soil.

Rocks have many sizes.

Rocks have many colors.

Rocks have many shapes.

Some rocks are smooth.

Some rocks are rough.

Some rocks are shiny.

What can you tell about these rocks?

Activity

How are soils different?

Look at three kinds of soil.

Which soil is found near your school?

How can you tell?

How are soils the same?

The earth has mountains.
It has hills and valleys.
It has flat places.

There is water on earth.
There is also dry land.

This map shows part of the earth.

Find the oceans on the map.

Find the land.

Find where you live.

How does water change the land?

Put some sand in a pan.

Hold up one end of the pan.

How will water change the sand?

Pour some water on the sand.

How did water change the sand?

Water covers much of the earth.

Most of the water is in the oceans.

Some of the water is in lakes and ponds.

There is also water in streams and rivers.

Water is used in many ways.

Living things need water to drink.

People use water to move things.

People use water to have fun.

How do you use water?

Water is important.

But sometimes people waste water.

Sometimes water becomes dirty.

What causes these things to happen?

How does water become dirty?

Put some things into different jars.

Label the jars.

Add some water.

Cover the jar.

What happens to the water?

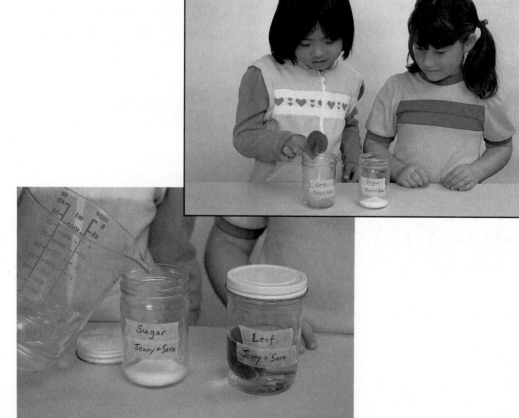

Air covers the earth.

We cannot see air.

We cannot taste air.

How do you know there is air in the picture?

Air is used in many ways.

Living things need air to live.

People use air to dry their clothes.

People use air to move things.

People use air to have fun.

Air can be harmful.

Sometimes air moves very fast.

Air can also become dirty.

How is the air in the pictures harmful?

Check It Now

WORDS TO KNOW

What are these things?

Match the pictures with the words.

soil   valley   rock   mountain   globe

Read each sentence.

Say the missing word.

water   oceans   air

Living things need ____ to breathe.

Living things need ____ to drink.

Most of the water on the earth is in the ____ .

126

IDEAS TO KNOW

Draw a picture about each sentence.

- The earth has mountains.
- People need water.
- Air can become dirty.

Water is used in many ways.

How is water used in each picture?

THINKING LIKE A SCIENTIST

Air can lift things.

Put a balloon under a book.

Blow up the balloon.

What happens to the book?

How is air lifting these things?

8

Looking at the Sky

The sky changes every day.

What do you see in the daytime?

What do you see at night?

How does the sky change?

128

The sun rises early in the morning.

It shines all day.

Sometimes clouds block the sun.

Then we cannot see the sun.

The sun sets at night.

The sky gets darker as the sun goes down.

Then we cannot see the sun.

The sky looks dark.

The sun is very important.

It gives us light.

Light from the sun strikes the earth.

Some of this light changes to heat.

During the day the sun warms the earth.

Look at the pictures.

How do you know light changed to heat?

The sky does not look the same at night.

We can see the moon and stars at night.

The moon is the biggest thing in the night sky.

It is smaller than the sun.

But it looks as big as the sun.

This is because it is closer to the earth.

How do things look
when they are far away?
Look at the size of a
bottle cap.

Move it far away.
Now how big does it
seem to be?
Did the size of the
cap change?

How do things change
when they are far away?

The moon does not give off its own light.

The sun shines light on the moon.

Light from the sun bounces off the moon.

The moon does not always look the same.

The moon travels around the earth.

We see only the part that is lighted.

The moon then seems to change its shape.

How has it changed in the pictures?

Why does the moon shine?

Go into a dark room.

Shine a light on a mirror.

What happens to the light?

Hold a ball in a dark room.
Does it give off light?

Shine a light on the ball.
Think of the light as the sun.
Think of the ball as the moon.
What do the light and the ball show?

People have walked on the moon.

They picked up rocks and soil.

They brought some back to the earth.

These things helped us learn more about the moon.

The moon is different from the earth.

The moon does not have air or water.

There are high mountains.

There are deep craters.

At night we see many stars.

Stars are like the sun.

They give off their own light.

Stars are very big.

But they look small.

This is because stars are very far away.

Some stars form pictures in the sky.
This is the Big Dipper.
What does it look like?

Check It Now

WORDS TO KNOW

Look at the pictures.

Match the pictures with the words.

crater   Big Dipper   day   night

   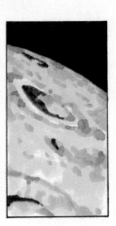

Read each sentence.

Say the missing word.

mountains   moon   heat   sun   stars

Some sunlight changes into ____.

The ____ is smaller than the ____.

The moon and the earth both have ____.

The Big Dipper is formed by ____.

142

IDEAS TO KNOW

Copy each sentence.

Which sentences tell about the sun?

Color a yellow sun after each one.

It gives us heat and light.

It rises early in the morning.

It shines in the night sky.

Looking at it can hurt our eyes.

THINKING LIKE A SCIENTIST

The moon seems to change its shape.

Look at the moon shapes.

Which ones are not shapes we see?

Put these things in order by size.

9

You and Weather

Look at the pictures.

Tell what the weather is like.

How does the weather change?

There are many kinds of weather.

Weather is always changing.

It can be warm or cold.

It can be wet or dry.

The wind moves clouds.
Clouds have many shapes.
What shapes do you see here?

Weather can change from day to day.

Weather can change quickly.

How is the weather changing in the picture?

How does the weather change?

Make a weather clock.

Try to guess what the weather will be.

Set your clock each day.

Change it when the weather changes.

How did the weather change?

spring

summer

fall

winter

Weather may change slowly.

It may change with the seasons.

There are four seasons.

How are the seasons different?

The air becomes warmer in spring.

Many plants begin to grow.

Many flowers bloom.

Summer days are longer.
The days are warmer too.
Plants grow bigger.
It is a time for summer fun.

In the fall the days are cooler.

Some plants stop growing.

In some places the leaves change color.

Then they fall to the ground.

Winter is the coldest season.

In many places it snows.

The days are shorter in winter.

Many animals sleep through winter.

Some animals have moved to warmer places.

You wear different clothes for different seasons.

You do different things in different seasons.

What seasons do the pictures show?

The season is the same in these pictures.

What season do you think it is?

How is the weather different in each picture?

Why is the weather different?

How do things change each season?

Make a season hanger.

Choose the season you like best.

Show things that tell about your season.

What changes did you show?

Check It Now

WORDS TO KNOW

What season is it?

Match the pictures with the words.

summer   spring   fall   winter

Read each sentence.

Say the missing word.

snowy   wind   flowers   season

Clouds are moved by the ____.

The weather changes each ____.

In winter the weather may be ____.

In spring many ____ bloom.

IDEAS TO KNOW

Look at the picture.

Name three things that do not belong there.

THINKING LIKE A SCIENTIST

Read the sentences.

Are there clouds in the sky?

Answer yes or no after each sentence.

It is raining hard.

The sky is full of bright stars.

You cannot see the sun at lunchtime.

10

Caring for Yourself

These boys and girls are in first grade.
They do many things each day.
They do things to stay healthy.
What do you do to stay healthy?

Tanya gets up early for school.
She washes her hands and face.
She gets dressed.
Her mother brushes her hair.

Eric gets up early, too.

Before school he eats a good breakfast.

This is what Eric ate today.

What did you have for breakfast today?

After breakfast Eric brushes his teeth.

Walking to school with friends is fun.

Tanya and her friends are careful.

They look both ways for cars.

They cross at the corner.

Eric rides the school bus to school.

He waits for the bus by the curb.

Eric obeys the bus rules.

He does not stand up in the bus.

He does not shout or talk loudly.

How can you cross the street safely?

Make a street on the floor with tape.

Make a curb.

Show where to cross.

Show how to get on and off a bus.

How can safety rules help you?

Eric and Tanya like to go to school.

They learn to read and write.

They listen to their teacher.

Learning is hard work.

It can also be fun.

What do you learn in school?

Your body needs exercise.

Exercise helps your muscles grow strong.

These girls and boys are in gym class.

What parts of their bodies are getting exercise?

Schoolwork can make you hungry.

Tanya buys her lunch at school.

Eric brings his lunch from home.

Eating a good lunch keeps you healthy.

Why are these good lunches?

Schoolwork can also make you tired.

Do you rest in school?

These children are having a rest.

Tanya has a snack when she gets home.

Then she goes outside to play.

Playing in the fresh air is good for her.

What do you do after school?

Now it is time for dinner.

Tanya washes her hands before dinner.

Work and play make Tanya hungry.

Tanya eats all the food on her plate.

The food she eats will help her to grow.

Why wash hands before eating?

Touch a potato with dirty hands.

Wash your hands well.

Touch another potato with clean hands.

What happens after five days?

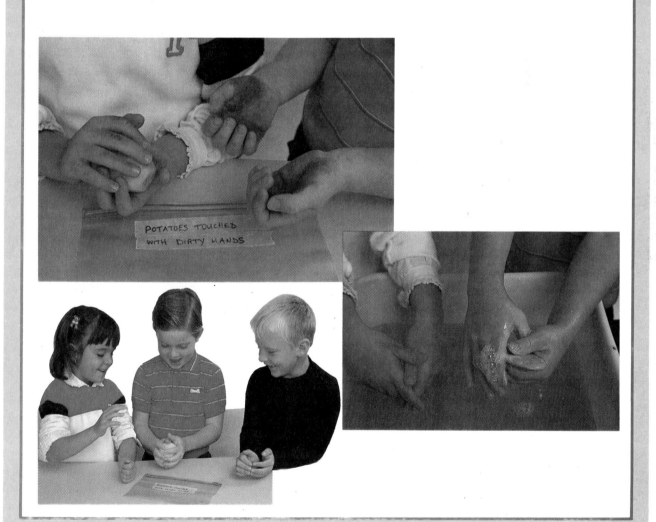

POTATOES TOUCHED WITH DIRTY HANDS

Healthy bodies are clean bodies.

Eric likes to take a bath.

He takes his bath at night.

He also brushes his teeth.

Eric worked and played hard.

He is tired from a busy day.

He will sleep about 10 hours.

Sleep helps his body get the rest it needs.

Tomorrow he will be ready for another day.

Check It Now

WORDS TO KNOW

Which meal is it?

Match the pictures with the words.

breakfast　　lunch　　dinner　　snack

Read each sentence.

Say the missing word.

hands　　muscles　　healthy　　brush

Before eating always wash your _____.

A bath keeps your body clean and _____.

Always _____ your teeth after eating.

Exercise helps your _____ grow strong.

IDEAS TO KNOW

Draw a picture for each sentence.

- Sit on the bus and talk softly.
- Cross the street at the corner.
- Walk with a friend.
- Play outside often.

Look at each picture.

Which ones show how to stay safe and healthy?

USING IDEAS

Eating out is fun.

Make a menu.

Draw healthy meals.

Science in Careers

People use science every day.

People use science in their work.

Science helps them ask questions.

Science helps them find the answers.

Science helps them do their jobs.

Doctors use science.

They help to keep us healthy.

Carpenters use science.

They measure.

They use tools.

They build.

Mechanics use science.

They fix machines.

They keep engines running.

Astronauts use science.

They study things in space.

Science Words

A

air Air covers the earth. You breathe air.

animal An animal is a living thing that can move on its own. A lion is an animal.

B

Big Dipper The Big Dipper is a group of stars that form this shape in the sky.

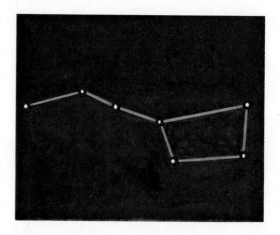

body All the parts of a person make up the body.

C

cloud A cloud is made of tiny drops of water. Clouds float in the sky.

colors Red, blue, and yellow are colors.

crater A hole in the ground shaped like a bowl is a crater. The moon has many craters.

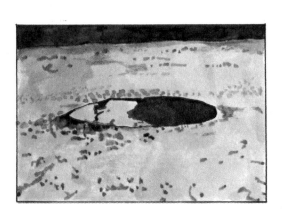

E

ears Your ears are the parts of your body that you use to hear things.

earth The earth is the planet where we live.

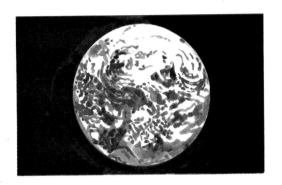

egg A baby bird grows inside an egg until it hatches.

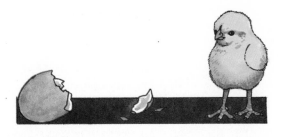

exercise Exercise makes your muscles work. Running and swimming are two kinds of exercise.

eyes Your eyes are the parts of your body that you use to see things.

F

fall Fall is the season after summer. During fall many leaves change color.

feathers Birds have feathers covering their skin.

flower A flower is the part of a plant that has petals.

fur Many animals are covered with soft hair called fur.

G

globe A round ball with a map of the world on it is called a globe.

grow When something grows, it becomes larger. People, animals, and plants grow.

H

heat Heat makes things warm.

I

ice Ice is frozen water.

L

land Land is the part of the earth that is made of rocks and soil.

leaf A leaf is the thin, flat green part of a plant. It grows on a stem.

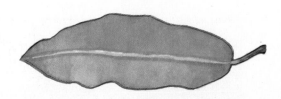

light Light helps you to see. We use lights to see in the dark. Plants need light to grow.

living things People, animals, and plants are living things. Living things are alive. They need food, air, and water.

M

machines People use machines to do work.

map A map is a picture that shows where places are.

moon In space the moon is close to the earth. At night you can usually see the moon in the sky.

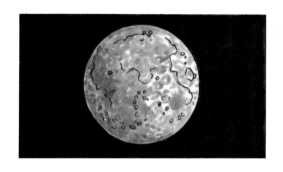

morning The morning is the first part of the day.

mountain A mountain is a very high hill. A mountain is higher than the land around it.

move Things that move can go or change place. Cars move.

muscle A muscle is a part of your body that helps you move.

N

nose Your nose is the part of your body that you use to smell things.

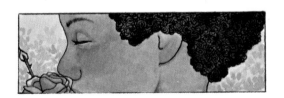

O

ocean An ocean is a large body of water. The oceans cover most of the earth's surface.

P

pet A pet is an animal that is taken care of by a person.

place A place tells where something is.

plant A plant is a living thing. Many plants have roots, stems, and leaves.

pull When you pull, you try to move an object closer to you.

push When you push, you try to move an object away from you.

R

rock A rock is a piece of stone.

root The part of a plant that grows down into the soil is called a root.

S

season A season is a time of the year. The seasons are spring, summer, fall, and winter.

seed A seed is a part of a plant that can grow into a new plant.

senses You use your senses to learn about things around you. Seeing, hearing, tasting, touching, and smelling are senses.

shape The shape of something is its form. A ball has a different shape than a box.

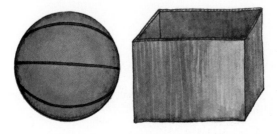

shell A shell is a hard covering. A snail has a shell.

shine Things that shine make a bright light. The sun shines on the earth.

size The size of something is how big or small it is.

skin Your skin covers your body. You use your skin to feel things.

sky The sky is the upper cover of air over the earth.

sleep When you sleep, you rest your whole body.

snow White flakes of frozen water that fall from the clouds are called snow.

soil The ground is made of soil. Plants grow in soil.

sound A sound is a noise you hear. A drum makes a loud sound.

space Space is the place beyond the earth. The planets travel around the sun in space.

speed The speed of something is how fast it moves.

spring Spring is the season when many plants begin to grow.

star A star is one of the objects in the night sky. Stars give off light.

stem A stem is the part of a plant above the ground that holds the leaves.

strange When something is strange, it is different or unusual.

summer Summer is the season after spring. The days are long and warm in summer.

sun The sun is the star closest to the earth. The earth gets light and heat from the sun.

T

tongue Your tongue is the part of your body that you use to taste things.

V

valley A valley is land that is lower than the mountains around it.

W

warm When we warm things, they become hotter.

water Water is found in oceans, rivers, lakes, and ponds. All living things need water.

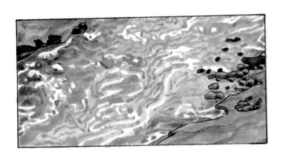

weather Changes in the air around the earth are called weather. Weather can be sunny, cloudy, windy, rainy, hot, or cold.

wind Moving air is called wind.

winter The season when the days are short and cold is called winter.

Credits

Cover: Michael Adams
Other Art: Leigh Grant, Rebecca Merrilees, Taylor Oughton, Ed Valigursky

The Adventure of Science A–B: Bob and Clara Calhoun/Bruce Coleman, Inc.; A–B m.: Grant Heilman Photography. A b.r.: Silver Burdett. B t.l. Silver Burdett. B b.: © S.J. Krasemann/Photo Researchers, Inc. C–E: Dan De Wilde for Silver Burdett.

Chapter 1 vi: t. Spencer Swanger/Tom Stack & Associates; b. Robert Frerck/Click, Chicago. l: t. Silver Burdett; b. Wendell Metzen/Bruce Coleman, Inc. 2: Silver Burdett. 3: t. Silver Burdett; m.l. E.R. Degginger; b.l. Alvis Upitis/Shostal Associates; b.r. © Guy Gillette/Photo Researchers, Inc. 4: Pensy Brown; inset Dan De Wilde for Silver Burdett. 5: Dan De Wilde for Silver Burdett. 6: Silver Burdett. 7: t. John Shaw/Bruce Coleman, Inc.; m.l. E.R. Degginger; b.l. G. Martin/Bruce Coleman, Inc.; b.r. Hans Pfletschinger/Peter Arnold, Inc. 8–9: Silver Burdett. 9: t. S.L.O.T.S./Taurus Photos; b. Steve Pradon/Taurus Photos. 10: b. Dan De Wilde for Silver Burdett. 11: t. Scott Ransom/Taurus Photos; m.l. Mary Bloom/Peter Arnold, Inc.; t.r. Richard Weiss/Peter Arnold, Inc.; b.l. Stephen Krasemann/Peter Arnold, Inc.; b.r. Lionel Atwill/Peter Arnold, Inc. 12: Peter Byron for Silver Burdett. 13: t.l. Pensy Brown; t.r. Peter Byron for Silver Burdett; b.l. E.R. Degginger; b.r. Craig Sherburne/West Stock, Inc. 14: Dan De Wilde for Silver Burdett. 15: t.l. Sal Giordano; t.r. Mary Bloom/Peter Arnold, Inc.; b.l. Thomas Houland/Grant Heilman Photography; b.r. Kenneth Fink/Bruce Coleman, Inc. 16: l., b.r. Dan De Wilde for Silver Burdett. 17: Silver Burdett. 18: t. John Running/Stock, Boston; b. Silver Burdett. 19–20: Silver Burdett. 21: Dan De Wilde for Silver Burdett.

Chapter 2 24: t. Alan Pitcairn/Grant Heilman Photography; b.l. Silver Burdett; b.r. Grant Heilman Photography. 25: t. Larry Lefever/Grant Heilman Photography; b. Pam Taylor/Bruce Coleman, Inc. 26: l. E.R. Degginger; r. Dan De Wilde for Silver Burdett. 27: S. Rannels/Grant Heilman Photography. 28: Silver Burdett. 30: t. Silver Burdett; b.l. Barry Runk/Grant Heilman Photography; b.r. Dan De Wilde for Silver Burdett. 31: Dan De Wilde for Silver Burdett. 32–33: t. E.R. Degginger/Bruce Coleman, Inc.; b. Silver Burdett. 33: Silver Burdett. 34: t.l. E.R. Degginger; b.l. Breck Kent; t.r. Eric Kroll/Taurus Photos. 35: Dan De Wilde for Silver Burdett. 36: l. © Gilbert Grant/Photo Researchers, Inc.; t.r. © Karlene Schwartz/Photo Researchers, Inc.; b.r. © Patricia Caulfield/Photo Researchers, Inc. 37: l. Harald Sund; t.r. Jacques Jangoux/Peter Arnold, Inc. 38: Silver Burdett. 39: t.r. Hickson-Bender for Silver Burdett; t. inset © Dan Guravich/Photo Researchers, Inc.; l. Breck Kent; b.l. Hickson-Bender for Silver Burdett.

Chapter 3 42: B. B. Richardson/Imagery; t.r. Richard Burde/Taurus Photos; m.r. E.R. Degginger. 43: l. E.R. Degginger; m. Robert P. Carr/Bruce Coleman, Inc; t.r. Don & Pat Valenti/Tom Stack & Associates; b.r. E.R. Degginger. 44: t. Wardene/Weisser/Bruce Coleman, Inc.; b.r. Peter Vandermark/Stock, Boston. 45: l. Bob and Clara Calhoun/Bruce Coleman, Inc.; b.l. R.S. Virdee/Grant Heilman Photography; t.r. Breck Kent; m.r. Scott Ransom/Taurus Photos. 46: t.l. Breck Kent; b.l. E.R. Degginger; t.r. Norman Myers/Bruce Coleman, Inc.; b.r. Grant Heilman Photography. 47: t.l. © J.H. Robinson/Photo Researchers, Inc.; m.l. © Russ Kinne/Photo Researchers, Inc.; b.l. E.R. Degginger; t.r. Breck Kent; b.r. James Carmichael/Bruce Coleman, Inc. 48: t.l. Jen & Des Bartlett/Bruce Coleman, Inc.; b.l. M.P. Kahl/Bruce Coleman, Inc.; t.r. E.R. Degginger; b.r. © Stephen Dalton/Photo Researchers, Inc. 49: t.l. Z. Leszczynski/Breck Kent; m.l. Frank Toman/Taurus Photos; b.l. E.R. Degginger; t.r. © Stephen Dalton/Photo Researchers, Inc.; b.r. R. Andrew Odum/Peter Arnold, Inc. 50: l. Stephen Krasemann/Peter Arnold, Inc.; r. © Bernard Wolff/Photo Researchers, Inc. 51: E.R. Degginger. 52: t., b.l. E.R. Degginger; b.r. Tom Brakefield/Taurus Photos. 53: Kim Taylor/Bruce Coleman, Inc.; inset © Walter E. Harvey/National Audubon Society Collection/Photo Researchers, Inc. 54: l. Fred Bavendam/Peter Arnold, Inc.; r. E.R. Degginger. 55: b. E.R. Degginger; t. Jacques Jangoux/Peter Arnold, Inc. 56: t.l. Fred Baldwin/Woodfin Camp & Associates; b.l. © Tomas Friedmann/Photo Researchers, Inc.; t.r. Stephen Krasemann/Peter Arnold, Inc. 57: Dan De Wilde for Silver Burdett. 58: Silver Burdett, courtesy St. Hubert's Animal Shelter; t.r., b.r. Dan De Wilde for Silver Burdett. 59: t. Linda Dufurrena/Grant Heilman Photography; b.l. E.R. Degginger; b.r. Cary Wolinsky/Stock, Boston. 60: t. Rosalie Larve/Bruce Coleman, Inc.; b.l. Silver Burdett; b.r. Alice Duncan/Taurus Photos. 61: Dan De Wilde for Silver Burdett.

Chapter 4 64–67: Silver Burdett. 68–69: Dan De Wilde for Silver Burdett. 70: Gene Ahrens/Bruce Coleman, Inc. 71–73: Silver Burdett. 74: © Lawrence Schiller/Photo Researchers, Inc. 75: l. E.R. Degginger; t.r. © Tom McHugh/Photo Researchers, Inc.; b.r. Leonard Lee Rue III/Bruce Coleman, Inc. 76–77: Dan De Wilde for Silver Burdett.

Chapter 5 80: b. E.R. Degginger; t.r. Silver Burdett. 81: l. Rod Planck/Tom Stack & Associates; t.r. Gene Ahrens/Bruce Coleman, Inc. 82: l. Stephen Krasemann/Peter Arnold, Inc.; t.r. Rodder/Peter Arnold, Inc.; b.r. © Michael Manheim/Photo Researchers, Inc. 83: © Leonard Lee Rue III/Photo Researchers, Inc.; inset © Jerome Wexler/Photo Researchers, Inc. 84: Silver Burdett. 85: l., b. E.R. Degginger; inset © Stephen Dalton/Photo Researchers, Inc. 86: l. Russell Bronson/Black Star; r. Steve Behal/International Stock Photo. 87: Dan De Wilde for Silver Burdett. 88: b. E.R. Degginger; t.r. © Gary Guisinger/Photo Researchers, Inc. 89: © Mike Lugne/Photo Researchers, Inc. 90: Silver Burdett. 91: NASA. 92: t. Robert P. Carr/Bruce Coleman, Inc.; t.r. Mary Bloom/Peter Arnold, Inc.; b.r. Jane Burton/Bruce Coleman, Inc. 93: Dan De Wilde for Silver Burdett.

Chapter 6 96: t. Silver Burdett; b. Jim Larsen/West Stock. 97: Bill Ross/West Light. 99: t.l., t.r. Dan De Wilde for Silver Burdett; b. Silver Burdett. 100: t. Timothy O'Keefe/Tom Stack & Associates; b. Douglas Miller/West Stock. 101: Dan De Wilde for Silver Burdett. 102: t.r. Mike Massachi/Stock, Boston; b. Stuart Allen/Black Star. 103: Silver Burdett. 104–105: Hickson-Bender for Silver Burdett. 106: l. E.R. Degginger; t.r. Owen Franken/Stock, Boston; b.r. Charles Gordon/West Stock. 107: Dan De Wilde for Silver Burdett.

Chapter 7 110: t.r. E.R. Degginger; m.l. E.R. Degginger. 110–111: b.l. Bob and Clara Calhoun/Bruce Coleman, Inc.; m.t. Don and Pat Valenti/Tom Stack & Associates. 111: r. John Gerlach/Tom Stack & Associates. 112: Silver Burdett. 113: NASA. 114: t. © Tom McHugh/Photo Researchers, Inc.; t.l. E.R. Degginger; m.l. Manfred Kage/Peter Arnold, Inc.; b.l. Silver Burdett; m.r. Barry Runk/Grant Heilman Photography. 115: Silver Burdett. 116: t.l. Robert Carr/Bruce Coleman, Inc.; b.l. E.R. Degginger; r. Dale Jorgenson/Tom Stack & Associates. 118: Dan De Wilde for Silver Burdett. 119: l. William Eastman/Tom Stack & Associates; t.r. Peter Arnold, Inc.; b.r. E.R. Degginger. 120: t.l., b.l. Silver Burdett; r. Clyde Smith/Peter Arnold, Inc. 121: E.R. Degginger. 122: Dan De Wilde for Silver Burdett. 123: Eric Carle/Shostal Associates. 124: l. Fred Lombardi/Photo Researchers, Inc.; b.l. Brian Parker/Tom Stack & Associates; b.r. Dave Woodward/Taurus Photos. 125: t. Brian Fox/Taurus Photos; b. Donald Dietz/Stock Boston.

Chapter 8 128: b.l. © J.H. Robinson/Photo Researchers, Inc.; r. © Russ Kinne/Photo Researchers, Inc. 129: r. Taurus Photos. 130: l. Harald Sund; b. Tom Stack. 131: Tom Stack. 132: l. Lynn Bodik; r. E.R. Degginger; b. Silver Burdett. 133: E.R. Degginger; inset Hickson-Bender for Silver Burdett. 134: Harald Sund. 135: Dan De Wilde for Silver Burdett. 136: Tersch Enterprises. 138–139: NASA. 140–141: Tersch Enterprises.

Chapter 9 144: t.r. Silver Burdett. b. E.R. Degginger. 145: t.l. Ben Sherman/Bruce Coleman, Inc; b.l. Edward Lettau/Peter Arnold, Inc.; r. Holt Confer/Grant Heilman Photography. 146: l. Charles Schmidt/Taurus Photos; r. Richard Perrine/Taurus Photos. 147: b. Gerald Corsi/Tom Stack & Associates; t.r. G. Cloyd/Taurus Photos. 148: Werner Stoy/Bruce Coleman, Inc. 149: Dan De Wilde for Silver Burdett. 150: Breck Kent. 151: b. Steve Raye/Taurus Photos; t.r. E.R. Degginger. 152: t.l. Glenn Short/Bruce Coleman, Inc.; b. E.R. Degginger. 153: John Shaw/Tom Stack & Associates; inset E.R. Degginger. 154: E.R. Degginger; inset W. Garst/Tom Stack & Associates. 155: l., m.l. E.R. Degginger; b. Charles Schmidt/Taurus Photos. 156: Stuart Cohen/Stock, Boston. 157: Dan De Wilde for Silver Burdett.

Chapter 10 160–162: Dan De Wilde for Silver Burdett. 163: Victoria Beller-Smith for Silver Burdett. 164: Dan De Wilde for Silver Burdett. 165: b. © Susan McCartney/Photo Researchers, Inc. 166: Dan De Wilde for Silver Burdett. 167: l. Victoria Beller-Smith for Silver Burdett; r. Dan De Wilde for Silver Burdett. 168: t. Dan De Wilde for Silver Burdett; b. Victoria Beller-Smith for Silver Burdett. 169: l. Dan De Wilde for Silver Burdett; r. Victoria Beller-Smith for Silver Burdett. 170: t. Dan De Wilde for Silver Burdett; b. Victoria Beller-Smith for Silver Burdett. 171–173: Dan De Wilde for Silver Burdett. 174–175: Victoria Beller-Smith for Silver Burdett.

Science in Careers 178: Silver Burdett. 179: b.l., t.r. Silver Burdett. b.r. NASA.

1 2 3 4 5 6 7 8 9 10–VH–95 94 93 92 91 90 89 88 87 86